D0922961

saint thomas. poems.

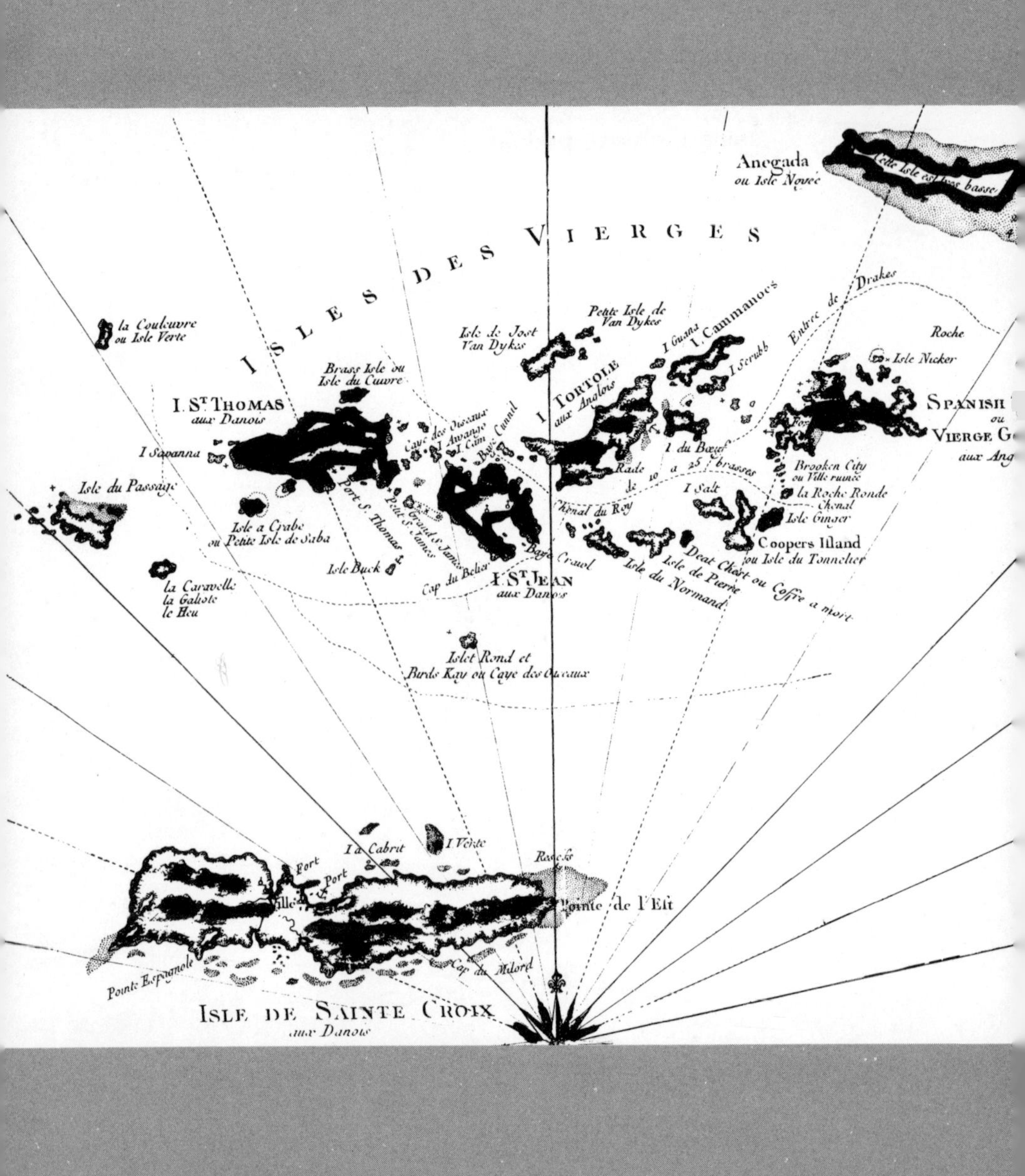
Anegada
ou Isle Noyée
Cette Isle est très basse
ISLES DES VIERGES
la Couleuvre
ou Isle Verte
Petite Isle de
Van Dykes
Isle de Jost
Van Dykes
I. Cammanoes
I Guana
Entrée de Drakes
Roche
Isle Nicker
Brass Isle ou
Isle du Cuivre
I Scrubb
I. TORTOLE
aux Anglois
I. St THOMAS
aux Danois
Caye des Oiseaux
I. Awango
I. Cam
Baye Cunnil
SPANISH
ou
VIERGE G
aux Ang
I Savanna
I du Bœuf
Rade de 10 a 25 brasses
Brooken City
ou Ville ruinée
Isle du Passage
Port S. Thomas
Petit S. James
Grand S. James
Chenal du Roy
I Salt
la Roche Ronde
Chenal
Isle Ginger
Isle a Crabe
ou Petite Isle de Saba
Coopers Ifland
ou Isle du Tonnelier
Isle Buck
Baye Craol
Cap du Belier
Isle du Normand
Isle de Pierre
Dead Chest ou Coffre a mort
I. St JEAN
aux Danois
la Caravelle
la Galiote
le Heu
Islet Rond et
Birds Kay ou Caye des Oiseaux
I a Cabrit
I. Verte
Fort
Port
Ville
Pointe de l'Est
Pointe Espagnole
Cap du Mlord
ISLE DE SAINTE CROIX
aux Danois

saint thomas.

poems.

tram combs

wesleyan university press
middletown, connecticut

Some poems previously appeared in *The Anagogic & Paiedeumic Review*; *artists boys cats : lovers judges priests / ceremonies in mind*; *Between Worlds*; *Bim*; *The Home Journal* (St. Thomas); *Marin Magazine*; *Mattachine Review*; *The Modern Poets: an American-British Anthology*; *One*; *pilgrim's terrace: poems american west indian*; and *San Francisco Review*.

Library of Congress Catalog Card Number: 65-14050
Manufactured in the United States of America
First Edition

for William Carlos Williams

saint thomas. poems.

the beauty of the many colors of your skins, St. Thomas,
lights me.
on any casual corner
i watch ever delighted the passage
of Indian – copper Borinqueños; black – black, purple – black
& brown – black Negros from down islands; native Euro – africans;
eggshell – pinks of pallid continents &, subtly swart, Semites
from Portugal & Spain, Poland & Brooklyn;
palest, "the poor whites of the Saints,"
& scatterings of Arabs & Asians.

•

a rill of jewels in a stream of Ind.

scent of jasmine
on the steep streets, & far be·low,
black water under blue stars

•

! nights of Charlotte Amalia !

principle plays in the movement of appearances. civilization re·forms in its monuments.

over Fonthill Abbey's stones
Beckford stared, near unbelieving,
through years of night
as workmen clambered the towers
like ants with hastening torches,
as his mad and civilizing dream of building
rose in the outward eye

the mid–night passes and i stare in trance
as multi·colored St. Thomas's teen–agers
twist and writhe in gusty gales
of light and sound from the juke–box

•

o
! deus in machina !
humanissima

•

twisting
their rhythms in verse

here am i a young man
sitting in my door–way as the sun re·turns
scratching dandruff from my eye–brows
and watching the animal rounds

i rose to bring paper and pen
to rescue kitty Camille yowling high in vines
and shifted to shadows
when the sun reached my eyes

i allow but these the sweeping clouds
cleansing seas, the sun and their leavings
only to move and move my eyes

soon all will be gone i've known
these forms when i lay down
i hug
this in mind

St. Thomas,
i have cast, broad–cast
you in my images
! how many !
gliding these airs down–like
or cleaving the waters shore·ward
will seek & see
you in my spirit

genesis

one wave
far off
on the stormy sea
struggles into flight

•

a gull !

among islands
a sailing boat
approaching the harbored,
slender, stately, and
rising chill like alien snow

take care with the terms
when you lend your – self to the city:
riot beauty it has, but not gentleness;
it demeans what it possesses. stand off,
anchor to water; have its skiffs come out.

bird noise

the prayers of the oyster–catchers
rise from their beaks
meeting the mussel,
shouting walking on the rocks, or
screaming a·wing onto the air
as man enters their arenas

palm poem

heave among stars
and grow like them

shake over us the sphere's tuning
catch and fleck us air's music, make light of it

be not stalwart but lasting through guile
assuage airs' violents by seeming following

mind's webs I find, shone,
filtering you sight and sound

re·flexions ·fractions

in the light when clouds are lit from below
the sickle – billed hummer buzzes the garden
at cactus bloom, hibiscus flower
and the lime's twigs, visited to sit on;
too the warbler
nervously compact
slips over – the – wall half – seen;
he cases the space
from half – a – dozen other – bird's eye – views.

•

the people in the street three feet away through walls
a • walk,
foot after foot,
had also reptilian ancestry
such as these

" a sudden wind has seized the cedar
and its flowers've showered pinking
the gray floor of this dull morning "

i wrote that twelve months ago
and remembered it just now
when, like lovers' voices in mornings,
tree and wind joined again

mating,

a dazzle of hummers
swirls our heavens
un·poemed
by
palm,
hibiscus bell,
or wave of caterpillar

those bloods
whose sense & thought
run slower,
yet

on a rim of the world

(with D. Clark)

a glimpse into the heart of things?
these flash–fires in the caverns of sun–set

light's last bead begins
orange, it burns to green & 's gone.

a moment of truth—
one truth—a unique one

just after noon with fierce shears
I set to at the hibiscus trees,
hacking away their under branches,
for a tunnel to study the mornings in.

then at the banked–up flower–beds—
withered iris out, down with vines dry for ten years—
sparing with care the life–lines of the daisies—
african, orange—
that plunge like comets from the spindling palm.

what a litter on the slates' dark–green!
rust cans, decay–gray'd paper, hunks of red brick,
wilting leaves—
I lean against the wall and all's silent.
and keeping the silence the lizards come—one two three

I see now, six, a dozen they crawl
on the rotted wood chunks, run along walls;
one springs to a vine and flows down it, another
peers 'round a sphere of pink lace.

the bared and dying all-ways of their world
they stare at, walk over.
once in a life
such wonder.

out in the morning
's subtle gold sheens
are hung the huge papaya planes,
slit, veined,
fly's – wing – like,
curled and feathering
in green maneuvers on the wind,
getting – on! with earth's mad whirl

showers !
of gold blossoming
fountain from its springing head alive
! a·live ! they spray
bees, -birds 'n us humming
with perfume 's to drown sense,
lead us toward its source

hymn

when I opened the door east
for dawn to come in
a small black hen
sped shrieking down the garden
and waddled the slope up
between beans and bell
peppers,
clocking like an ocean
under the moon before the sun

(greek poem)

like a weathered ancient ship, the island
lifts into the storm;
clouds swirl on its mountains,
our flags flap, and
stars and our far lights in the driving
windy rains flicker

now our nests of shaven wood
hold warmth for us, hold
our skins from moisture not from within

the street stones ! gleam !
air is cleansed, dust's
returned to earth;
in the pour of water, fire
extinguished, but for this
fifth element, intelligence

peopled hill scene night

which is the last
light of earth
/ the first
of heaven?

past noon it rained
after parching months

and in the night
great – mothers of wood – lice swarm
tumbling on long wings into wider lives
after life times long in attentive waiting
guarded in halls of birth

•

how many of their attendants died there the while
eying their heavens like our ancient Egyptians
toward this event?

on a wave·let of the millennium

•

but a thumb – nail of moon
dresses the living to-night
birds and night – blooming cereus
cry out softly in the shards of light
lovers more gracefully gesture
under its flattery

•

our light is going out & will return

the young lizard lashes his tail at the universe
like a lion – trainer his whip.

i called him young; but the word sounds odd
for him so much older than we
(it seems more a link in a named chain
than an individual un·related, as we conceit our-selves)

I wonder at their deaths;
I've never seen one's body in the patio;
protected from their enemies — large birds, animous reptiles,
all but age and bacteria — they must be slowed by one,
stopped by the next, and die in the crevices of
these walls;
and lie, lie, hourly entering more
and more into the life of ants
and worms and the air.

in the stormed grass she
lies and the waves glint and assault her

she lifts her nose, tenses her eye – lids
and smiles as the wind riffles her fur
spearing it as does rain:

I spoke her name from the door – way

young mosquito, I Love
and yet struck you —
your flesh's mangled
and movement's one fitful leg

I remember Jains wandering on India
with gauze at their nostrils
so not to destroy
any fellow feeling being

signals of Pain race your communications.
with my thumb I stop them.
murmur Absolution.

old – time torturers told
of philosophy therewhile

bite me, willya?

the anarchist in town

the butterfly knocks cheerfully
along the maze of men's streets

it's not that he thinks our ways;
there's just less in his way that way.

the two cats cool in the window
watch me
—ice–green eyes
in polar–bear hair

& beyond:
the hill–top sour–sop fruit,
hibiscus bloom,
& mustard & pink
the walls of the tropical mammal
man
's town
rise
for the happiness of eyes

thus
this world flowers
& i must

Mutual Aid, Columbine

is harmones and melody, rolls and wine
of our lives: I rill your ribs by thumb
and you murmur to me like a mandolin.

now among our delights very great
is Columbine, brief cat, rich
dark browns with gold and glints of cream

when the sun's over Hawaii and we come home
she, a moon–shadow on the earth at the ridge
slips to our feet and darts home away
always just before; bend to touch her
and she spurts on minnow–like

pick her up to caress
she thrusts you away and twists to jump

in morning's pale hour I am wakened
among surf–sounds from trees
by the happiness of cats; Columbine on an oval
woven rug
sits and sounds her pleasure. I touch her fur;
she moves intensely under my fingers

dawn

when I stepped first on the chill floor
I learned Bathshebo last night had eaten
the bottoms of the socks I wore too long.

greater love hath no cat.
he was sick in the dining room.

I flung up my arm half from sleep,
my fingers dangled past the bed
—onto the dark house, minute
slivers of stars down spheres of air're
bounding and drifting gently to earth
into the elephant ears' darknesses
and waiting buds of hibiscus:
the house ! swirling, laced in them—
past the bed's edge fingers fell
and a soft rasp attached to them, a cat's tongue,
file of love.

I drew back,

and thought deliciously of the dark presences
amorphous · tiny
two black kittens
back of the couch
in the next room
with enormous blue eyes
wondering
stillnesses

this is the puzzle in physics for the kitten, appearance
suddenly of fingers lancing the swollen light
with yesterday's associations
of various fun

& the technology how
to make the most of it

(rooms rivers jewels eyes)

deep blue – luminous bowls
to meet your siamese eyes,
Bathshebo, I've bought for you
unnecessarily

that time's wounds and promises
to our little rooms
will coalesce and go
as your subterranean – rivers – lit
jewels at such jewels move

the intellect

pink nose, moist lip,
eyes seeking correspondence —
the entire cat – machine
is working full – steam this morning,
i discover, looking about,
after i've had coffee

Timba, all pinks and pales,
forlorn is sitting on the
gray of this floor and
we regard each other.

thus, Timba, led by your nose,
shell ear, fox teeth and eyes like
caves of glass i
move, encircling seven times hell.

my feet are dusty.

i sit on the floor
having given my bed to a friend.

thus, holding each to a mute companion
the philosophers
mused the tiers of love.

this odd puppy assembly
of bones, meat and skin
smells the world and waggles.

grace with time's going will come
& you'll have then less to charm us;
swing, baby, at every hour.

st. thomian dogs sense in – common strong
one will bark
in the back of the night
the first faint light
(or any hour but sleepiest sun-light's)
and answers like ! shots'll
ricochet
wall to wall, valley to valley
how their ! volleys roll . . . .
over this old
rock . . . .
wholly, wholly . . . .
wholly . . . .

un · american dog

Olé ! the honey – colored cocker
shares our hunger for excitements
but his are not Sade · istic movies,
quick guns more thorough
after sex in books
but the shadowy figure in the garden be · low
'ranging before dawn
coffee – pot and poems
—
thief of a dog's imagination

you're my own animal,
Santos Celosos,
so far as possession goes
between forms so different:
you yawn, smile, proffer
that ever–dirty nose,
eat fish and horse, shed hair and shit,
speak to strangers
insisting on answers,
and add a hundred happenings a day
to this quiet mind
that seeks toward truth
and some integrity to things,
at least as much
as fragmentizing mind can find,
and founds symbolic crystals of its news;

are you distracting?

no; no.
mind can use you
as well as fallen deer, leaf or priest,
as bow to string
core to collect on
gun to run

in this mystical abstract
race
nowhere
without opponents.

bearing

Ish cat -child, wild,
the infant you've dropped, all ginger and cream,
cocoon – shaped and squirmy in the garden thicket
worms up in instinct in your
loving fur womb – warm,
under your gold eyes star·ing through the fern-
fronds laced with quick – silver oils of sun

first birth — in calmer times, Tiger·Ish,
you're shy of me, a few quick steps off all ways
but to-morning after this night / wilderness, wilder
when the streams of the Creator tore you
you look to me with strange hungers / love

cradled by the Creator we re·turn
to our fellow creatures
new – eyed

a stone yard for you cats to be, to be
safe from the savage, boy or dog,
and the rush, crush on the cars' road

meats o' morning, milk in the twilight
and my breezy bed with the human smell
to lie on; fellow feeling in my voice and hand

at nine – twenty the new cat —
black – dotted white cat —
hopped into the box once more

she entered the home last night
and the box to-night
and quick she chose it

before her it housed water – white liqueurs —
squat dark bottles
with slim necks like clams

in her last pregnant hours
Two – Button sits swaying on her paws
belly wine – skin – shaped
braced on earth

stoned by dreams
— o' the flower seeded within her —
coming to altar
their fluids of home

your substances and muscles moving strange
— Two – Button, we only can watch
you, help · less — mind nebula'd awash
alone now in that great current

cat – mind ages

over a vision of bronze patriots,
topping the coral – wall, centuries old
the kitten licks, sits, peers round
at every eddy in the ambience

dark & pale the angelica greens
tremble lightly in the dusky heat

as his mother, a'stalk,
gray like modulations of the grass, has eyes
only for bird – flesh, scattery in the trees,
not for people, stones or leaves

what is this passion to join our fleshes,
Victoria, that tense you nuzzle my arm – pit,
scrub ears and chin at ankles and thumbs

when first you arrived
such fury for contact all night long
I got no sleep till I threw you out

now after breakfast six months later
I find I cannot type with the window open:
with glad cries It erupts with Victoria
leaping to mingle fur and fingers,
arch the back, squirm, turn, utter heart murmurs

life's brief hours never will be enough
to still, satisfied with stroking, this
white fur, ring – tail, nor for smiling into your
blue eyes,
Victoria, these desires, sweet cat of these seas.

even when you're among the dead I'll remember
throwing open these windows mornings
I find you coming through the patio
crying stirring the pale lights here to me;

you give this earthly flesh
in conscious waves against my
probes and messengers of affection fingers
rumbling in cat delight;

I'll hope in that manner of dreaming then
you will have found
a friend in that new form
who'll be affecting for you thus.

I was not with you when you died, Victoria,
and that last stormy clutch at consciousness
I heard far down your growls
and wondered what enemy had entered the house

•

not with jewels, not with perfumes,
not with Testaments
lay i you in your final grace
but unadorned turned to your mother / Maker: self

•

chin up, legs running for
the house of love 's feeding calls

• • •

this poem's then your winding-sheet, Victoria;
like wine from soil-centuries of grape-leaves —
your trans·forms long-going begun —
you go clothed from us in this frame

David — chocolate ears, oaten fur
and blue eyes on the green bed – cloths –
in our symbiosis thus

I view your de•bris on the bed – sheet
with mixed emotions —
flea – halves, cast claw – sheaths, flea – shit
and your hair, dirty paw – prints —
all the furniture of the personal nest / re•pose
from the licks, jerks, bites
of life and your toilet

you fill into adolescence and the
flares about you grow more luminous;
in the nights and tense forests on your
skin I see sleek fleas swim.

it's mine too, this labor
from / (to) love, toward maintenance:
I scratch the dirt out and crush your fleas
where you've not learned to

you have grown up in the ways of this house,
David, it's stepping in through the back
window and scratching by the telephone,
new lights from the butcher next door each morning,
lording it over all the cats in the neighborhood, and
purring silkenly out to greet me when I come home,
has made you you.

from your youngest days
arriving, snatched from mother
infant – terrified, it has been here you've been,
in here you've grown.

and we must leave it now

sweet company in the world's odd ways

what terrors await you in new homes
next – door dogs, giant cat cannibals —
sleeping forever on corners where man's approaches
and beasts' are signalled
in time to wake / attack / run
years till death's total quiet

Nada Mas,

an artful friend
arrives to curl
on the yellow straw rug
orange, white & black
hair immaculate
ex·pressing interior harmonies

•

sympathy antipathy apathy
(?)

table & chair, animal & friend,
thoughts in print,
all delights of the mazy mind.

cats' indifference is a shallow manner,
designed to conceal.
leave a while.
they'll be racing or waiting
round the place of your going;
enter; & they walk away.

the table glows
pathetic to cut & burnishing
as friend shapes to the artist's hand,
or chair, pet, fine–painting....

•

& this re·conceiving
of the colored kitten.

Armistice Day
or daily

they do not accept you as a cat, sweet cat;
their plebiscites make no arrangements for you.

when will you learn to appear human?

it is necessary,
to survive
among these predatory or under–simple
who make the state up–most.

society

mingle your ginger
hair my cats
among the golden
of the children

suffer them,
christianly,
& remember
it's better to be mistreated than ignored

what in the elfin
momently sightless
world under the sink
as I shave has
watery–brushed my bare leg?

only Africa
fresh in flipped-
shivery, from sudden rain
re·assuring soul
through flesh

books

with one paw largesse to Webster
Columbine lazes a long after–noon;
yester–evening the Mabinogion rolled with her slumbers;
and this morning she shinnied me up and
dropped her ass onto 'sui generis'
in Kenneth Burke.

ah Columbine Columbine, though you are youthful
(six weeks) we differ little: I too I suppose
favor them slightly over pillows or gardening soil
for life's long hours;
let us fare together on this earth.

among the whites of houses
on a black horse down hill
slowly a white – shirted rider winds
— on his chest the whiteness fluttering
at his wrists the sleeves billowing —
among the palm and banana fronds feathering,
massy trees floating on
the wind coursing his path

earth – round

(for the McArts whose garden it is)

over the city a
house – wife leans wheeling wheeling
sheets into the morning dripping

they ! sail ! streaming from the racing
ring of earth into light — their wet flanks ! gleam
as the winds of whirling belly them

through our thin seas
white WHITE ! WHITE !
over the violet garden

lovely to see man the lively up–right
animal thinker walking
& his works

launching on seas below his house
whirling starward in the airless
rolling on wheels he's motored
naked in gardens
cloth'd on his streets

drunk
in winds of morning / wines of divining
i greet you—

! yes !
stoned by these antique delights
& attending those arriving

down fields of concrete a negro boy running
running, running and near him grasses are springing
under the sun the bronzy brome
seeds burnish suddenly as his dark foot passes

dropped to this city, this estate

's this your response
weeping to stand
at the gate without trousers?

some are hailing the streets
with lyrical feet
toes and tips all swaying
like flames in time
but you stand here in tears

but well; they are not vehement nor balanced
live with life's fervors pleasures
who've not some – times
cried at gates without trousers

hood, seven –

(Binky's)

how can it be thus shot – like through the air
(more often than not just after dinner
— us adults lying about, digesting)
firing from the middle of the floor
onto the couch with louder – than – indian cries
(the Indians after all were grown – up;
they couldn't have hoped to compete)
there must be some discernible technology
to this boyness, being all essence of
mindless menace all – at – once, at seven
that we can learn and ruin
(lovingly)

the savage and flower
opens and shouts
at the ice – box:

! boy !

•

yeh. how to
take the bloom off
shut it up

yes, let us be at building, boy,
life's library of experiencing
the things never to touch, do;
pretend never – to – see
all these coming – on -young years

but pity your elders, less resilient
do not be donkey – bitten
black – & – blue – banged scooter / tumbler,
marble – swallower
all in one day, again

•

this too's to learn:
moderation

! pink kite !

sprite in the sky !
or spirit !

of the boy
who cannot fly
but thus

bather

you will have
that peach – flesh flesh
so brief a time

wrap it
if wrap it you must
in metal – green mesh,
narrow
the loin – form forward

that we
stepping near you on the sands
may start · to dream and remember
why we are here

I *knew* when I swung
with those tangerine thighs
it was great

now in the night's recoil three years later
I've climbed from bed to record it

thus
making that buoy again

to an aloof young man

I heard in a dream last night you'd shipped
as cabin–boy on a freighter to Spain,
and one of your duties was running
soup–kitchen for twenty–six crew.
what delight! I recalled it again
and compared last year
when you refused to face
hard facts and get down to work.
exquisite revenge!
I'll mail you this.

St. Thomas,

your yard of graves
i find
bound round
with bars & whore–houses.
thus
the city goes,
well
-rounded, -founded

damsel from down islands

Tina was a beauty when she first struck town
the night's thousand eyes all
swung when she subtly shivered,
' the juke-box jumped, the competition lost
all, always, shout as it might

the bar-tender at Mike's she cut to size
(he looked askance at her beat-up sandals)
by calling for 'beer' in selected tones,
and, from her diving neck-line lifting
fifty bucks, one bill, to cover the tab

unfortunately else-born, the U.S.'s guardians
shipped her off, they said
(they lied)
she was an undesirable alien, when
all they really meant was somewhat un·american

one Bostonian Indies – gone

watching you bolted in cloth
glittery translucent scarlet
swishing the female essence
like a perfumed smoking censer
    —I find I cannot believe this;
    closing my eyes I see you in teen–age dreams
    switching in South Sea grasses ankle–length

        a lady's courtesies go only so far
        before leaving the name
        get off the floor
        you must be reading my mind

    five centuries have swung these isles
    to european and african foot.
    but I can see you too in dreams of history
    shifting leisurely through the fields
    hispaniolan rolling fern
    caroling odd, Taino
    among the maidens of Anacaona

we return;
turn on

the sexual gestures of plants
shake out their sails in the winds of sunlight

as do ours
traced to the moon

gym

under slender cylinders, radiant like radio – towers
of white light on naked walls

on upward ranks of bare poles
on rings, tracks, before pneumatic bags —
resonant, leaping at – a – touch —
young men move in abstracts

their muscles tighten like fruits
trunks're swung, flung, lift,
limbs asterisk'd, swastika, fall
like sail lines in strange winds

among bars of wood, bars of light
lank ropes, cables, rings, sensitive spheres,
trapezoids, deltas,
on stuffed horses, broad pads

with guitar or machine – gun, the stuff of dreams
the boy addresses him – self to the universe.

Angel · us
on an in · carnation

he won't last
won't keep that beauty
nor will you
admiring
always desire.
make it, man,
while you may

time runs and turns
as do we
and our Gods
creations
changelings

as you find it
now not for – ever;
dive;
strive

Indianapolis idyll
something to move with

keep to mind how among golden lands and
light–houses of children in plays of
fountain and sun
we voyaged and lifted in calms of love
and high beyond the city went down
to range in the moony night in
the springs and herbiage
of our faces, limbs and dells, salt and sweet.
I called out to you: we'll never forget this
it's one of the great nights
and in your hands you rolled my head,
contemplative
cup filling
falling a·drown
in
the light
splashing uproariously
now through openings of God.

Love,
such celebrations of the flesh
in unrest of spirit
you & i have made
rest mind & body both to-night

i love ! you
as i told you,
then & now.

•

& will in the night – mind's courses
send in mental swings
your name / my cries
in thanks & praise,

Love !

an aid to life,
the sight

of this handsome young man
who poses on corners
all eyes
caressing the passers – by

& if he's offering his sexual services
so much the more

rising from your breast
my slowly – withdrawing eye
finds all my wiry hair
impressed there

& should some miracle suddenly hold
that vision for eyes distant in time
(like those old old footprints filled with rock)
the thoughtful ways behind those eyes might run
'one creature gestured to another thus'
or
'thus they clung
cold in the tropical noon
seeking warmth from each other'

last at night and in the earliest light
your long eyes, and resin laugh
are live in the bed here

(like waters' fall in the mind's mountains
storms, stars, burning beasts of seas,
gods in lacquered niches)

I dream your arms and pits,
in the strands of sleep
mould you — toes, thighs, tongue

after coupling

horns from the fog off San Francisco
oceanic rains assaulting St. Thomas
tree – frogs in Puerto Rico
snow – nights' quiet
leaf – drop in deciduous falls
:
how many sounds have i wakened to?

—

shoulders hung on
faces turned toward
•
i'd
lighted
roused
burned
•
on

how many nights will you feed
before the death you seek?

bruised blue from the last rough trade,
stoned for four days

the boy who loved you best
left you but years of despair

we turn in the sun but briefly
and under – ground long

now we have you among us
i walk by your side a·live

take your hand, i may,
go with you a way

lover:

I stand in, steal from
you that figure of yourself
you cannot make

28.

no longer quite so beautiful
or young your love of self looks back now
and friends, surprised, are led
into those pleasures your fantasies
no longer exercise

ill health and squalor
self portraits and hunger
among; and a legend that love's the central
reality you go unreal

•

but, friend; not less that desolations lead you
to these new eyes for me
suddenly without you my life's lonelier

we do affect each other —
a cat cannot ignore another cat —
' re·present yourself
by the enemies you accept

sketch

(for Girard & Aarone Premel)

like a black quartet
by Cezanne out of Gauguin
Negros move dominos
in the Cinderella Bar
down & far out
in the muddy slums

at the Join Right Inn on saturday nights
the girls sing raucous and the
boys pelvises swivel their
hips neat in low – slung pants and
belts tilting down – belly

brazen girls wear no brassieres and startle sailors;
the boys sit on impatient testicles,
dart looks;
two girls are hopping
to Cha – cha – cha

antillean

Anacaona's angelic voices
choired the Spaniards
into the forest

as you, sweet lady,
shouting from the juke – box
lead us thus in ways of bliss
we shall not keep
—
the dime's worth gives out

those who go for sex
've left before four;
the bar – keep circulates rousing / raising
the unsuccessful
slumped in the toilet,
asleep on the couch

daylight's the time of the idea'd Christians'
far – out concepts
and their police
relax at night

the genre seen is part of God;
here's the relax, cradled – in – laps
morality -play

sailors on liberty

no responsibilities and small thought, dictated to,
clocked to breakfast, crap and sleep, chastity,
they sprout handsome
hair–horns, come on impish
shining–faced and eyes merrily
untrammelled, ready to break rules.

the town's stones patter as they foot–fall it.
their bars buzz with whores and boiler–makers;
they get belligerent, bloody each other,
shatter windows, stone the world with
bottles, chairs, urine; go back sick,
relieved a little. weeks of routine;
controlled; being told; they'll be back.

ship – mate

on the sailor's stern
twin screws are tattoo'd
& under his keel
"steer clear"

as the Russians' mirrory cannon–ball balls through space
the Sputnik Cocktail appears on the drink–list
at Pierre's Diner

(sloe–gin and soda–water)
new compartments of man begin;
the buck must be turned

like elegant cake or a palace in·vision
in pink and many blues
The New Lulu's Tavern
arises on the sight from
ordinary soil along–side Main Street

chords of juke–box re·sound from its shell
crystally laces of iron fret gracefully the doorways
and tiles sheen the personality;
inside go people, sprawling at tables

its sweet nut–meat is Lulu
looming in the kitchen
dark with her dark cat Tram,
denizen of affection
feeder of dozens of fellows

1953 gestalt

'the pains of lizards'
I started the poem,
seeing a cat   savage one,
de·tail and skin its back

but arrested I heard
friends' voices say
'the pains of lizards!   and China dying?'

the lizard's inched from sight now
under the wax–vine flowers and I,
by this pink wall record the actual:
Norman is ill three feet away
and Carol changes jobs today
for ten pieces more toward life's expense a month;
xylophone little–boy tones
ring these airs and walls

greed

too clever at retention
of a tenth of the land surface
is this family, otherwise near–cretinous

•

a living apologia
for the ceremonial stonings of China

gargoyle

he dreams of gracious living midst declining
capitalists of the '20's in their 70's —
peacocks and hounds, ball-gowned ladies and
altered servants.
he rushes over the streets
like a barrel with legs
in white shorts, ashy cigarette;
rooms he approves he enters loud.

captain o captain

his idea of a 'high old time'
is racing through the city in
taxis talking of his 'very intelligent wife'
and shining up for every cunt unmanned
! romance, synthetic and intense

but his home on the deep his
every-night life
is the first mate's back
even in port,
tide up!

the poet

sits there
waiting to be raped
by the muse
& hoping
it won't come out a bloody mess
again, like last time

once a year?
he can bring it off
howling in
the breath of life

be wary of spare hours
and thought with vitals;
the uni-verse is not rigged
for such storms.
idle minds addle.
they may find you crumpled
in a bath–tub, in a shark,
under a castle of Spain or the air,
belted and saddled with gold in Africa,
or ad·justing in a London counting–house.

on Saint John, divine
in the desert   by Veneziano

John, in massive italianate youth,
with the grace of usual gesture
lays away his red cloths and stands
not concealed against us, universe

in his loins   but a few years have swum
the flowers of life, cells of maleness springing,
that universal we ride on, river, driver, deriver
so nearer untimed than we, that wears us, that
vanishing swifts, we're borne by, bear

among mountains stone of the Immaculate
imagined, delicately firred, marvelous
on a pebbled deck, he stands alone

•

odd to–night that, sleepless at four,
I should have drifted onto you.
for days I've been turning returning to
phrases and images for a poem on
buddies moving through such Sierras
stopping long after noon to wash, fish,
make–it and vanish into sleep in the meadow–grassed
face of God as sun
was slung off, and the mountains rushed holy
into coloring wondrous into fine shadows
and darknesses of horn'd–moon night

christian song
for us crossed on Christ:
of God
cut down and re·shored

for the pleasures of raisins, cheeses and wine,
chicken in pinot and smiles at table,
strolls and conversation at three, star–lighted,
the sweets and sounds of bed like strings in
orchestras of forests or Java, cups, rung,
and our costumes, dawning and sun–setting
self–fettered in gold, limes, blacks' pale–blues,

Christ! you have lamed us
your sallow mind and followers'
visionlessness, violence.

and all the delicate sweet shocks out–of
darknesses as lights break in us—
as the sun–light new now through the window
north·ward the red wall's dappling—
we come not with these, rising in your name.

but for the hour on the mountain lone with God,
our dedications purposes martyrdoms,
for our deaths magnificent
you are, and our deaths are daily—
myrious–netting the separations among men, dogs, cedars,
our selves in the streaming
world / time.

(continued)

through humility you rose from all – we children out of God
almost beyond us in legend; but still as person,
legend, institution powerful cripple.
though it's easier to die, to let
others dye us than to live
stalwart I's in labor,
death signs awe – full to the simples of us;
and a hundred generations after
your name and body, racked to heaven's lights and desires
ring us in continually.
from your personal days you were
out most the palings of our fires.
all – times we'll liven at your name,
live, listing to your halts, blindnesses;
but let us move on up a little higher,
tooled with the powers / potentials of your thoughts and life,
elaborate, balance & tune us to essences and entires
of each and our groupings, our structures, desires —
to any's, alls of us — by / to these notes, measures . . . .
but 'wilder when we have the harmonics:
Christ!

good friday

it was this day
his passion reached its crisis, clearest
just after the sun stood highest
they rocked the spikes
into his hands and hauled him
ankles also bound
into the sky
to die

•

all the ways of that elevation
we can not reconstruct now,
but if only to know
there once was so noble so graceful a hastened
going as to forgive
its ignorant acters there their ignorance —
here, in our own ways
crossing this
is an aid

church cross verse flesh

as Dorothy Day says
"the church is *our* cross
for crucifying Him"

•

precious young dreamer / dream
so long a·dying

& those little stirs in life
when we young in enthusiasm rush Him:
"don't go!
God has but we shall never
forsake you, fellow!"

yet & ever he hangs on
/ in these scraps
of breath, & us
weeping & raging
about the applications
of these potentially moving feet

for Alice Wallace

near one's hundredth year the world beats softer
the storm in the tamarinds awes now with gentleness
the visitor; and one's chickens cry softly;
rain falling drops more quietly
into the brimmed pan.

the grave's but a little lapse
when movement and breath 're so slight;
how far from their riots when, sixteen,
a youth to a country picnic
asked for her dancing and began
proper court; they wed
and divided to nine;
or the lyrical night in an ankle–long gown
all white she waltzed, waltzed, spinning down boards
laid in a maze, and missed never a step.

near the hundredth year one's desires quieten.
tea in the after–noons; and occasional fine candies;
visits from one's children, even unto the fourth generation;
visits from neighbors;
little gifts to them.

my eyes open in wonder.

it was of your flesh, mother,
i first was made;

now i watch its dying pains.
o, that i might
give back that gift.

life swings on in widening gyres;
it is not ours,
but with it we're;
our grace goes in adjustments.

come here we hardly know how
we watch, act, we
cry out and go
from these masques masked each other.
yes, thus we smile.

for a lady
lately dead, buried at sea

that gravel–rolling voice, Antonia, will be heard again
any time some one of us turns a corner of your haunts.

who else, pot–bellied and spindly–shank'd, will
liven our mid–night hours with total balls!

leering at the sailors as you pranced and turned,
empty beer–tray poised on the head—oh most lady–like

slender toe neatly so lifting and, all the while
that cackling, sinister and obscene; we adored you.

none, certainly, had escaped your insults and attacks.
but those who'd cursed you hardest wept the most.

your body refused and refused, they say,
to enter the sea; and some say too that swimmers

ever after, nearing your sea–deep sepulchre
will hear the voices not of angels but of 'Tony

in the heaven of her carousing; and i do hope so.

the occasional splendor of evening
light in calm flight from God
to sun, cloud, sea & man

•

stirs in mind again those ancient awes
that we are, sense & continue;

such geometries we divine
arise in mind's stores to events of sense.

•

new acts – of – art! / -of – mind! we seek
who beat it ever on
toward cliffs of the new
experience & perception

•

how how in those e·lusive flights—
!ware, !ware—to form, feather, per·
·form, ·fect in place & constant act
this reluctant animation

inter·pret with letters
to some perfect in – sensation
these matters in day·ly flight:
(among)
root, leaf, fruit & man, light & god

aware aware

that corner of earth
where i beat to death
some dozen of those oozing creatures
that feed on the garden's rottings
haunts me

they, too, sentient, Buddha–like, felt
and i hurt them

•

perhaps, though, it's the fresh un·life there
i sense that troubles me;
certainly my pangs to them were brief

cast here pyramidal we fleshes compete
for space, to feed each on others greens—
our grace co·existence with mutual aid there–toward
(in dry summers Thoreau would
(water the wood–land orchids.)
and he's most graceful in the butchery
who's most aware
all's done there.
in these matters in space of our meetings
we 'rive to acts below the mind's potential visions.

(continued)

animal cannibal creature born we strive to rise
by our mind's unsettling
lifts and ecstasies,
struggles
we re·vere to this
actuality we
find our–selves a·part in, unable to understand,
but lift from our closes competing
wolf, ant, mouse;
and, flesh–eaters, will eat flesh—
thus to this race
in these our circuits temporary

we who have sought some form
of correspondence with God

return.
sighing.
no.
nothing.
it's not there.

all this is so no–where.

when i met Nyogen Senzaki*
he served sweet cakes & fine tea.
"gifts," he said,
"wrong
for a monk to buy,
but equally wrong to refuse as gifts."

"do you eat meat?" he asked
as we walked out to feed.
"yes."
"so do i," he said;
& we fell upon a fellow-feeling fish—
plank'd & grill'd, basted with soya sauce
hot from fires;
he was delicious, we agreed,
feeding in delight.

the first zen monk resident outside Japan

to H.D.

this house in the western Indies carves
the storm to its very form
closeting dry these man – grown leaves
freighted with poems
of honey dripping from over – ripe pear
bird – attended, flower scarred from salt
sand – drift, and some summer storms
of bees — all those beauties
uncountable, uncontrollable
dreaded and delicious
of your Mediterranean — ever summer,
ever alive with great loves

catch to us in sweet chains Greek
girl, odd bird, sea – growth, great tree —
sculpt for the singing
presses many seed-
poems yet to be wing'd
to shelter in such attending shells /
soil, and grow

ars poetica about ultimates

when you first rub up against God's own skin
He turns out to be rougher than Christ's men
most expect,
like a wood – rat, -rasp or ravenous
connoisseur with tender grapes a rough trade!
yet this seduction and adoration
of Him we must get done, dangerous
though it go: poetry's ways're
strewn with the early – de • railed, • ridden, • filed who
heard its sirens; and rose to go
singing, but couldn't make it, hammered
and strove but with beats unsuccessful
to get on to come on with
the real jazz and sea for one's
self, to reach follow •, fellow •, father •
ship with Him!

you dig Suzuki,
Radhakrishnan and Christ
and have nothing to say?

in a century of change

it's a cold meta·physical wind blows
with this sudden and chill
april rain.

i think on the dark ages of man
we struggle from, yet here,
so near at hand.

perhaps its swirling shifts re·mind us of our deaths;
the drops, unthinking where they fall,
're im·personal, but in vagary.

yes, it's cold here;
and i turn and go, under
the garden's drenching blossoms to the house.

the soft whirr of its machinery
coming from the door with light
is subtly comforting.

—the nacre! the shell that lines the creature's lair
lends to such grace as thus far we've got—
coffee–pot, cold–box, machine–made fire.

to Him

out of these tears, terns' crashes, creels
we cry out cry out
Lord, Lord!: we make thee Lord
build and unfurl banners to you
set out marches where thy sway sounds shallowest

come!
to be!
among!
us!
in

·spiriting

as we walk
in the offices
of thy day:
in red, chartreuse and earthen,
blackbirdy golds,
other roles,
but only for thee
' go

elegy
on the community of the living

in the wind of years
our monuments de·face—
those features so sweet to us
we cut, cast
in such care
loose & leave us,
watch or not,
the gods go,
a mere millennium
at Angkor
& their faces
ruins by roots

•

& was it, thus, waste?
no.
while they were
we were.

(mystic / scientist / poet:)

God speaks with an as·tonishing stammer.

•

it's all this figuring—
his speaking out

the mystic is gone

dazed
he watches
days go
as rain–bows
in God's eye—
isles, clouds, heads—
arc
in
passing

all about us lie poems of God but who can understand them?

Index

THE WESLEYAN POETRY PROGRAM

Distinguished books of contemporary poetry available in cloth-bound and paperback editions published by Wesleyan University Press

Alan Ansen:	*Disorderly Houses* (1961)
John Ashbery:	*The Tennis Court Oath* (1962)
Robert Bagg:	*Madonna of the Cello* (1961)
Robert Bly:	*Silence in the Snowy Fields* (1962)
Tram Combs:	*St. Thomas. poems.* (1965)
Donald Davie:	*New and Selected Poems* (1961)
James Dickey:	*Drowning With Others* (1962)
James Dickey:	*Helmets* (1964)
David Ferry:	*On the Way to the Island* (1960)
Robert Francis:	*The Orb Weaver* (1960)
Richard Howard:	*Quantities* (1962)
Barbara Howes:	*Light and Dark* (1959)
David Ignatow:	*Figures of the Human* (1964)
David Ignatow:	*Say Pardon* (1961)
Donald Justice:	*The Summer Anniversaries* (1960) (A Lamont Poetry Selection)
Chester Kallman:	*Absent and Present* (1963)
Vassar Miller:	*My Bones Being Wiser* (1963)
Vassar Miller:	*Wage War on Silence* (1960)
W. R. Moses:	*Identities* (1965)
Donald Petersen:	*The Spectral Boy* (1964)
Hyam Plutzik:	*Apples from Shinar* (1959)
Vern Rutsala:	*The Window* (1964)
Louis Simpson:	*At the End of the Open Road* (1963) (Pulitzer Prize in Poetry, 1964)
Louis Simpson:	*A Dream of Governors* (1959)
James Wright:	*The Branch Will Not Break* (1963)
James Wright:	*Saint Judas* (1959)